EVERY

with

FOR GROWING

CW00665824

THE WAYS OF
GOD

BY SELWYN HUGHES

QUIET TIME

Great King of kings,
we build elaborate
temples of hope to house You –
carve ornate and costly
imaginings of
how You shall rule in this
big needy world ...
and have absolutely no idea that
Your eye is fixed upon our
small needy hearts.

Susan L. Lenzkes

"IT'S HIS WAY"

For Reading and Meditation: Exodus 33:1–14

*"... the Lord would speak to Moses face to face,
as a man speaks with his friend ..." (v. 11)*

There is no doubt in my mind that one of the most significant and important lessons the Lord desires to teach us, is a deeper understanding of His ways. The more we understand God's ways, the better we will get on with Him, and the richer will be our relationship with Him. Once we begin to look at our circumstances through this particular lens, life takes on a completely new perspective. It changes from boredom and emptiness, profitlessness and purposelessness, to meaning, direction, hope, encouragement and deliverance from despair. I clearly remember situations when, if I had been better acquainted with the ways of God and knew them as well as I do today, many frightening circumstances would have been robbed of their terror.

THE LEISURED HEART

After I gained some insight into the way God likes to do things and came to terms with it, I entered into the experience of what someone has described as "the leisured heart". Those who knew me well said: "What has changed you? You were fussy, aggressive and easily ruffled – what has made the difference?" I had the joy of telling them that I had begun to understand something of God's ways, and with the understanding had come a deep inner security and peace.

In Psalm 103:7, we read: "He made known his *ways* to Moses, his *deeds* to the people of Israel. The Israelites knew only the deeds of God and easily fell prey to murmurings and misunderstandings; Moses knew the ways of God and became, as our text for today shows, His confidant and friend. Some see only the actions of God: happy are those who understand His ways.

Happy are those who understand His ways.

My Father and my God, I know you have put your finger on something that is important and significant – my need to become more familiar with Your ways. Help me come through to a deeper and clearer understanding of this. For Jesus' sake. Amen.

"WILL YOU BE MADE WHOLE?"
For Reading and Meditation: John 5:1–15

*"When Jesus saw him lying there ... he asked him,
'Do you want to get well?'" (v. 6)*

We ended yesterday by saying that many are living strained spiritual lives because they do not understand their Father's ways. Thus they do not know the experience of the "leisured heart".

THE BEST EXAMPLE

Jesus, of course, is the best example of what it means to live life in the knowledge and understanding of the Father's ways. He was never in a hurry, never ran, was never worried or flustered and appeared to be adequate for every situation that confronted Him. In the passage before us today, we see He was so familiar with His Father's ways that He quietly walked past the crowd of desperate people sitting by the pool of Bethesda and said to just one person: "Do you want to be made well?" Why didn't He ask that same question of everyone? There was a great multitude of people needing His help – why focus on just one?

I used to have great difficulty with this passage until I came to see the connecting links in verses 17 and 19: "My Father has been working ... and I have been working ... the Son can do nothing of himself, but what he sees the Father do" (NKJV). Jesus seems to be saying that He did not get His guidance from what went on around Him, but from what went on above Him. Note the phrase – "what he sees the Father do". Jesus looked up to heaven, saw that His Father's way in this situation was not to heal all but to heal one, then moved in to make the divine will a reality. The way of man would be to minister to the whole multitude, but God's way was to single out one individual and focus only on him. But why? We can speculate but we do not really know. Suffice to say – it was His way.

He was so familiar with His Father's ways.

Father, help me to understand that though Your ways are sometimes unpredictable, they are never capricious. There is always a good, gracious and benevolent reason behind everything You do. Amen.

IS GOD IRISH?

For Reading and Meditation: Isaiah 55:1–13

"As the heavens are higher than the earth, so are my ways higher than your ways and my thoughts than your thoughts." (v. 9)

The incident we looked at yesterday points to the fact that God's ways are so different from man's that they sometimes appear to go in opposite directions. We have a certain approach to life – but God has another. And unless we come to terms with this, we will find a lot of the things that go on in our Christian life make no sense at all. A friend of mine from Northern Ireland claims he can prove from the Bible that God is Irish. When asked to support this claims, he says: "Because God does everything in the opposite way to everyone else!"

CONTRARY TO POPULAR OPINION

In one of my seminars, there is a section where I go through some Biblical passages which show how some of God's ways are directly contrary to man's. For example, man thinks that leadership is getting others to serve us. God says: "Whoever wants to become great among you must be your servant" (Matt. 20:26). The great are not those who have the greatest number of servants, but those who serve the greatest number. Then again – man thinks to surrender his life to God is to lose it. God says otherwise: "Whoever desires to save his life will lose it, and whoever loses his life for my sake will find it" (Matt. 16:25, NKJV).

Take one more example – man thinks that the basic keys to good health are sleep, food, exercise and rest. A phrase often used in today's newspapers and magazines is this: "You are what you eat." God says that "godliness is profitable for all things" (1 Tim. 4:8, NKJV). Sleep, food, exercise and rest are important, but not half as important as a godly spirit. It is not so much what you eat but what is eating you that is important.

God's ways are so different from man's.

O Father, I see how opposite my ways and thoughts are to Yours. Help me bring my wandering desires and inclinations into line with Your perfect will. In Jesus' Name I pray. Amen.

REVEALED – NOT DISCOVERED

For Reading and Meditation: Romans 11:25–36

"Oh, the depth of the riches both of the wisdom and knowledge of God! How unsearchable are his judgments and his ways past finding out!" (v. 33, NKJV)

Already we have begun to look at some of the specific ways in which God works, but before we proceed further we pause in the light of today's text to ask ourselves this question: if God's ways are "unsearchable and past finding out", why try to discover them?

The point this text makes is that it is impossible for the human mind by its own ability to search out and understand the designs of the Almighty. It is not saying we cannot understand them; it is saying that we cannot understand them by our own unaided reason. In fact, God has graciously condescended to let us know something of His ways through Scripture, and one of the main purposes of the Bible is to help us become familiar with the Almighty's habits and methods of working. So without any further preamble, let's dig into Scripture and see what we can learn about our Father's ways.

STANDING THE TEST

I have selected for our meditations over the next few weeks eight specific ways of God, and the first to come under consideration is this – it is the way of God to test before He entrusts. God will never place us in a position of great responsibility in His Kingdom without first putting us through a series of spiritual tests. The apostle Paul said: "Because he counted me faithful, putting me into the ministry" (1 Tim. 1:12, NKJV). A. S. Way translates it thus: "He tested me ... ere He entrusted me." Believe me, if you want to do something great for God, then you must be willing to be tried and proved. And the testing is not so much that God might be convinced of your ability to perform, but that you yourself might become more refined and ready through the process.

Willing to be tried and proved.

O Father, help me understand that I must not look upon Your tests as obstacles I have to overcome, but as opportunities to be grasped. For I see that it is as I grapple that I grow. Amen.

HE IS LOOKING STILL

For Reading and Meditation: Mark 12:35–44

*"… he sat down opposite the treasury, and
watched the multitude putting money into the
treasury …" (v. 41, RSV)*

Yesterday we said that everyone who seeks to do something great for God must be prepared to undergo a series of spiritual tests. What are some of these tests? I have discovered, both in my own life and in talking with others, that there are five or six major areas of testing, which God uses before He entrusts us with special responsibility in His Kingdom.

One is the money test. Our text tells us that Jesus "sat down opposite the treasury, and watched ..." I believe He is watching still. I remember very clearly, in the early years of CWR, when just hundreds of pounds went through my hands, how the Lord spoke to me and said: "I am watching how you handle this responsibility. Do it well and I will give you greater things to take care of for Me." Later, as CWR grew, thousands of pounds went through my hands, and again the Lord came alongside me and said, in the tenderest way: "I am still watching."

ONE OF THE SADDEST THINGS

I made mistakes, of course, but they were not major ones and were easily rectified. Now, along with my fellow directors, I am a trustee of property which is worth close on two million pounds. One of the things I find saddest is to see a young man start out in the work of God with tremendous spiritual potential and then fail the money test. I know some Christians, and so I am sure do you, who looked as if they were going to set the world on fire, but because they couldn't handle money – they fell by the way. It is a sobering thought, but our Lord still sits quietly by the treasury, carefully watching how we handle money and the influence and effect it has on us.

Because they couldn't handle money – they fell.

O God my Father, I see so clearly that money can be a ministry or it can be my master. Help me see that I am a steward, not a proprietor, and that everything I have is part of a sacred trust – Your trust. Amen.

THE TIME TEST

For Reading and Meditation: Colossians 4:1–18

"... make the very most of your time."
(v. 5, Moffatt)

We continue looking at some of the tests which God uses in preparing us for special responsibility in His Kingdom. Our Lord sits alongside us, not only to look at how we use our treasure, but also at how we use our time. One of the greatest tests of discipleship is what we do with the minutes and hours that are entrusted to us day by day.

I am convinced that if I had not learned to become a good manager of my time, I would never have been able to continue writing edition after edition of *Every Day with Jesus*, which is now read by hundreds of thousands of people around the world. In the words of John Wesley, that master user of time: "Never be unemployed and never be triflingly employed."

THE REAL PROBLEM

In photography, we are told that the picture depends, not only on what you put into it, but what you leave out. Your capacity to say "No" determines your capacity to say "Yes". You have to say "No" to lesser things in order to say "Yes" to greater things. "Life", it has been said, "demands elimination as well as assimilation." That is why the first qualification of a writer is – a waste paper basket. Throw away things that do not contribute.

Time is distilled opportunity.

Can you pass the "time" test? Do you carry on conversations, for example, long after they have run out of intelligence? Or waste hours daydreaming? Time is distilled opportunity – a sacred trust. Don't waste it, for in doing so you waste yourself. People often say to me: "My problem is that I don't have enough time." I usually reply: "No, that's not your problem, your problem is that you do not use to the best advantage the time you have."

My Father and my God, I want to be ready for whatever You have for me in the future. Help me make the most of every moment, so that when the great moments come I will be a prepared person. In Christ's Name I ask it. Amen.

BE A FINISHER

For Reading and Meditation: Luke 12:35–48

"...'Who then is the faithful and wise manager, whom the master puts in charge of his servants ...'" (v. 42)

Another test which God uses to prepare us for special responsibility in His Kingdom is the persistence test. Talk to any spiritual leader you know, and I will guarantee that somewhere in their life, you will find that God brought them to a time when they felt like giving up – but kept going nevertheless. The Church is filled with people who made good beginnings but bad endings. Louis Untermeyer, in one of his prayers, said:

> From compromise and things half done
> Keep me, with stern and stubborn pride.

PERSEVERING TO THE END

One translation of the passage before us today says: "Where is the trusty, thoughtful steward whom the lord and master will set over his establishment?" Note the two words "trusty" and "thoughtful". A "trusty" servant will go through to the end, a "thoughtful" servant will consider the best ways to achieve that end.

Some time ago I watched a marathon race on television and saw a man come in hours behind the others. As he staggered toward the rope, weak and exhausted, the crowd applauded him more than they did the winner. And why? Because although he finished last – he finished. Everyone is impressed with a finisher. In 1 Corinthians chapter 16, the apostle Paul said: "I am staying on ... I have wide opportunities here ... and there are many to thwart me" (vv. 8 and 9, Moffatt). Many others might have said: "I am quitting ... I have wide opportunities here ... but there are too many things against me." Determine, whatever God asks you to do, that you will stay with it – and finish it.

Determine that you will stay with it.

My Father, I know You want to use me. But I cannot be used unless I am trusty and thoughtful. Help me to be trusted to go through – clear to the end with unwavering persistence. Amen.

THE "WHAT IS" TEST

For Reading and Meditation: Philippians 4:8–20

"… I have learned to be content whatever the circumstances." (v. 11)

We continue looking at some of the tests which ,God puts His people through before He passes on to them greater responsibility in His Kingdom. Today we look at what I am calling the "what is" test. I am thinking here of those Christians who adopt the attitude: if I were anywhere but here, I would be all right. They dream of what they would do if they were not in their present circumstances. They are like birds in a cage, uselessly beating their wings because they cannot fly.

LIVING IN THE HERE AND NOW

It is true that we must have vision in our Christian experience and we must not stop desiring and longing for higher things, but we must never allow the desire for "what can be" to hinder us from living effectively in the "what is". The children of Israel lived on manna in the wilderness as they journeyed to the Promised Land. Imagine it – manna every day for forty years! They got tired of it at times, but it sustained them right through the wilderness journey until they got into the Promised Land.

You and I may get tired of our present circumstances or situation, but we must learn to live with it until we get to our Promised Land. If I was to tell you the difficulties and problems that we encountered in remodelling Waverley Abbey House, you would have difficulty believing it. We might never have stayed with it if God had not taken us this way before and taught us the lesson of living with the "what is" until we come to the moment of "what will be". If we can't get what we like, then we must like what we get. Learning that lesson gives us staying power that transforms everything.

We must like what we get.

Lord Jesus, You who lived on the manna of the silent years of obscurity in Nazareth – and lived on it gloriously – help me to live on the "what is". Then I can really live. Amen.

UNFIT FOR DUTY

For Reading and Meditation: Psalm 141:1–10

"Set a guard over my mouth, O Lord;
keep watch over the door of my lips." (v. 3)

Today we look at another test that God gives His servants before He entrusts them with special responsibility in His Kingdom. This one has to do with that part of us which is comparatively small but causes so much trouble – the tongue. Many a person has ruined a church fellowship as well as shipwrecking their own spiritual future through a wrong use of the tongue. The expression of a thing deepens the impression of it, so a word uttered becomes a word made flesh – in us. In other words – we become what we express.

THE TONGUE IS A FIRE

I knew a man whose spiritual potential was so great that the college at which he was trained considered him to be a second Billy Graham. He took charge of a church and for a while things went well, until one of the church members offended his wife. Instead of taking the person to one side and dealing with it on an individual basis, he chose to lash the whole church with words that were un-Christian and uncharacteristic. The church said: "He is not the man we thought he was: nothing can justify such an outburst." They lost confidence in him and today the man is in the spiritual doldrums – shut out of the ministry because he could not control his temper or his tongue.

Be assured of this – before God elevates anyone to a higher and more advanced ministry, He is going to say the same as your doctor sometimes does when he examines you for some illness – "Put out your tongue." If it is a tongue that is stained by unrestraint and indiscipline, then He will have no other option than to regard you as unfit for duty – though not cast out.

We become what we express.

O Father, help me grasp the point that a word uttered becomes a word made flesh – in me. For my words will condemn me to be what they are; I become the incarnation of what I express. So save me from an undisciplined tongue. In Jesus' Name. Amen.

"FOR CHRIST'S SAKE"
For Reading and Meditation: Ephesians 4:20–32

"Be kind and compassionate … forgiving each other, just as in Christ God forgave you." (v. 32)

The forgiveness test is another way in which God tests us before entrusting to our care great spiritual responsibility. Some time ago, while dining with a group of ministers, I was asked: what do you think is the biggest single factor that causes spiritual shipwreck in the lives of God's people? I hesitated, for many things sprang to mind – jealousy, dishonesty, impurity, prayerlessness, etc. – but one thing stood out above all the others: an inability to forgive.

UNWILLING TO FORGIVE
Over the years, I have been privileged to listen to the secret concerns of Christian leaders as they have sought coun-selling for their problems, and time and time again, I have heard them say this: "Someone has let me down badly and I have been deeply hurt and offended. I find it almost impossible to forgive." I have heard this same story in many parts of the world from men and women who were on the threshold of a great ministry in the Kingdom – ministers, missionaries, evangelists, elders and so on. I had to tell them that unless they could pass the forgiveness test, they would not go much further in the work of God.

Take my word for it, if you want to do anything for God, then come to terms with the fact before you start that you are going to get hurt. People will disappoint you, tell lies about you and vilify you – so prepare for it by learning to forgive. And the secret of learning to forgive is to do it "for Christ's sake". You may be unable to forgive on your own, but with His help and by the breath of His Spirit, the impossible becomes Him-possible.

The biggest single factor that causes spiritual shipwreck.

O Father, You know the difficulties I have in forgiving those who have hurt or offended me, so help me to be willing to be made willing. Take my willingness and add to it Your power. With You, I can do anything. Amen.

ARE YOU IN BONDAGE?

For Reading and Meditation: Proverbs 3:11–26

"My son, spurn not the Eternal's schooling ... his discipline is for the man he loves ..." (vv. 11 & 12, Moffatt)

The final test I would like us to look at is that of un-disciplined desires. Many are ruled by desires that they cannot control and thus they disqualify themselves for an important role in the Kingdom of God. It has been said that "the future of the world is in the hands of disciplined people". I would go further and say that the future of the world is in the hands of those who know how to discipline themselves to the demands of the Kingdom.

RIGHT DESIRES WRONGLY USED

Desires are the God-given forces of the personality and as such are right. Physical desires such as food, drink, sex, etc. are natural desires, but when they are undisciplined they become a hindrance rather than a help to the Kingdom. Take food, for example – some Christians are in bondage to what is known as "comfort-eating"; they find their comfort in food rather than in their heavenly Father. Then there is the subject of drink – many are in bondage to stimulants and alcohol. Dare God entrust us with spiritual respon-sibility if He sees that we don't know how to keep a clear head? For remember – what is in the stomach often deter-mines what is in the head.

Take also the subject of sexual desire – a powerful force that can drive us to accomplish great purposes or drive us on to the rocks. I am sure that everyone reading these lines now will know of someone with a promising career in Christian work who has come to a sudden stop because they let their sex drive run away with them and entered into an illicit relationship. As one preacher put it: "John the Baptist was not the only preacher to lose his head over a woman!"

Many are ruled by desires.

Heavenly Father, help me to harness all my desires and to drive them in Your purposes, for if I don't – they will drive me. I am a servant or a master. Let nothing master me – except You. In Jesus' Name. Amen.

WHEN ENTERING A TUNNEL
For Reading and Meditation: Psalm 119:25–40

*"Let me understand the teaching of your precepts;
then I will meditate on your wonders." (v. 27)*

We turn now to consider another "way" of God – those seemingly strange and unpredictable actions of the Almighty which baffle human intelligence, yet have a wise and benevolent purpose running through them. God sometimes guides us in a certain direction and then appears to abandon us, leaving us to struggle and flounder in the most difficult and discouraging circumstances.

This particular "way" of God can be summed up in this phrase – He reveals, reverses, and then restores. First God reveals His purpose, then after a while proceeds to reverse it so that it looks on the surface of things that He has abandoned His original intention or changed His mind. Then, at His own appointed time, He brings the original purpose to pass in an unmistakably supernatural manner.

CAN GOD BE TOO LATE?
God revealed to Abraham that he would become the father of a great nation. Abraham was in no doubt that God had spoken to him, and by faith set out on a journey to an unknown destination. Later, the revelation God had given to him appeared to go into reverse when it became obvious that Sarah, his wife, was barren. But the Almighty reaffirmed to Abraham that from his body would spring a nation that would be more in number than the stars of heaven (Gen. 15:5).

Sarah had passed the age of child-bearing. It looked like God had left things too late. God's revealed purpose seemed to have gone so far in reverse that it could never be restored. But that is precisely how He delights to do things.

He reveals, reverses, then restores.

All the great acts of God have behind them this principle, and the more acquainted we are with it, the more secure and confident we will be when the train of divine guidance leads us into a dark tunnel.

O Father, how can I ever be grateful enough to You for showing me through Scripture the wonder of Your ways. Burn deep within me the consciousness that all things proceed according to Your plan – even when they go into reverse. Amen.

PRISONER TO PRIME MINISTER

For Reading and Meditation: Genesis 37:1–28

"… his brothers pulled Joseph up out of the cistern and sold him for twenty shekels of silver to the Ishmaelites …" (v. 28)

Yesterday we saw how the principle that God reveals, reverses and restores was illustrated in the life of the patriarch Abraham. Today we see that same principle illustrated in the life of Joseph. "For colour and kaleidoscopic effect", said Dr W. E. Sangster, "the story of Joseph ranks with the 'Arabian Nights' and is one of the most moving narratives in the whole of Scripture." Who could disagree?

RESTORED IN GOD'S TIME

When Joseph was a young man, God revealed to him through a dream that he would play an important part in the plans and purposes of God. But not long after the revelation was given, it suddenly went into reverse when he was sold by his brothers to some slave traders on their way to Egypt and finished up a slave in Potiphar's house. I wonder what Joseph thought to himself during those hard and difficult days as a slave in Egypt. Did he ponder on his dreams and question the reality of God's message to his heart? Whether he did or not we shall never know, but one thing is certain – the revelation that seemed to go significantly into reverse was, at God's appointed time, most wonderfully restored.

Let me remind you of the events that brought him from being a prisoner to Prime Minister. Promoted, in the passing of time, to overseer in prison, he became renowned for his ability to interpret dreams. Then, in the momentous hour when he solved the perplexities of Pharaoh's mind, he stepped in one mighty stride from being a prisoner with a few privileges to the Keeper of the Royal Seal with an authority second only to the throne.

The revelation was most wonderfully restored.

Gracious and loving heavenly Father, as I see this divine principle so clearly illustrated in Your Word, help me to recognise it just as clearly when it is at work in my own life and circumstances. In Jesus' Name. Amen.

GOD'S WAY OF PREPARATION

For Reading and Meditation: Exodus 2:11–25

*"… 'Who made you ruler and judge over us?
Are you thinking of killing me as you killed the
Egyptian?'…" (v. 14)*

Today we see the same principle at work in the life of another Old Testament patriarch – Moses. First God revealed His plan and purpose to him, then reversed it and finally restored it.

A SENSE OF DESTINY

When Moses was a young man, he became deeply concerned for the plight of his Hebrew kinsmen who were in bondage to Pharaoh. Did God reveal to him at that time that he was to become the one who would lead His people from slavery to freedom? There is no verse of Scripture that says this, but I think it safe to assume that there was rising within Moses a sense of destiny and an awareness that he had been saved from death for a divine purpose.

Most Bible commentators feel that the verse which says: "After Moses had grown up, he went out to where his own people were and watched them at their hard labour" (v. 11) suggests that there was forming within Moses' mind the conviction that he was there for a divine purpose. Doubtless his mother would have told him of the promise which God gave Abraham that one day, the Hebrew nation would be brought into a land flowing with milk and honey, and also have acquainted him with the ways in which God had supernaturally preserved the people of Israel.

So although we cannot say for certain that God revealed to Moses that he was to be the deliverer of His people, I believe myself that his conviction was forming in his mind. Assuming this to be so, then no sooner did the God-given idea arise than it went into reverse. Following the murder of the Egyptian, Moses was rejected by his kinsmen and forced to flee into the desert for forty years.

There for a divine purpose.

My Father and my God, I am grateful for this daily exposure to Your Word. Help me see that this truth which is confronting me is not a whim of Yours but a way. Reveal it to me even more clearly, dear Lord. Amen.

ENDINGS AND BEGINNINGS
For Reading and Meditation: Matthew 26:57–75

"… he went in and sat with the servants to see the end." (v. 58, NKJV)

WEEK 3 DAY 1

Today we look at a New Testament example of how God reveals, reverses – then restores. When Jesus was here on earth, He began His ministry by announcing the news that He was in the world to establish a kingdom – the Kingdom of God. Listen to how Matthew puts it: "From that time on Jesus began to preach, 'Repent, for the kingdom of heaven is near'" (Matt. 4:17).

THE SUPREME EXAMPLE
Throughout the three and a half year period of His public ministry, Jesus put before men the dazzling prospect of a kingdom in which He was the rightful King. Multitudes responded to that message and, at one stage, so successful was the atmosphere surrounding the Son of God that some of His disciples began to argue about who should sit at His side in the coming kingdom. It seemed to them that Jesus was about to oust the Empire of Rome and become the King of Israel.

At the end of His public ministry, however, the revelation of the coming kingdom suddenly went into reverse. The Saviour was brought before His captors and treated like a common criminal. Simon Peter thought, as our text for today suggests, that this was the end; the things that Christ had said about the coming kingdom were nothing more than a dream. The revelation Christ had given concerning the Kingdom of God was seemingly at a point where it could never be restored. Who ever survived a crucifixion? But three days after His death on the cross, God miraculously raised Him from the dead and restored to the dispirited Peter, as well as the rest of the disciples, the truth that had first laid siege to their hearts.

The truth had laid siege to their hearts.

O Father, help me understand that when the revelation You have given me goes into reverse, it is not the beginning of the end, but the end of the beginning. Thank You, dear Father. Amen.

REASONS FOR REVERSALS

For Reading and Meditation: Zechariah 4:1–10

"... 'Not by might nor by power, but by my Spirit,'
says the Lord Almighty." (v. 6)

Having examined this principle over the past few days, we now ask ourselves two questions. First, does God allow this same pattern with all His revelations? And the answer is, No, not all of God's leadings follow this pattern – but the major one's always do.

Secondly, why does God adopt these strange and mysterious methods of working? He does it because there is just no other way that He can bring about His perfect purposes.

IN HIS TIME AND WAY

When God reveals something to us, He knows that we have within us a combination of godly concerns and human perspectives. We are eager, alert and full of natural enthusiasm, the things that help us get going to do His bidding. But a moment has to come when our natural enthusiasm is overlaid by divine perspectives.

God allows us to go ahead in the strength of our own eagerness and then, at the appropriate moment, He puts things into reverse. When we come to this point, we see that if the revelation that God has given us is to be realised, it will not be because of our strength and prowess – but His.

When we learn that lesson, God miraculously intervenes to restore His purposes. Note the word "miraculously". The fact that things are restored miraculously is a constant reminder that God must always have the biggest part in a project. In that way, no onlooker can be in doubt as to who is responsible for the success – everyone recognises it to be God. If things are in reverse in your life at the moment, rest assured – God knows what He is doing. The vision will be restored. It is His way.

God must always have the biggest part in a project.

O Father, the way You reveal and restore is so exciting – it's the middle bit I don't like. Yet I see I have to go through it if Your purposes are to be worked out in me. Help me to remember this the next time things go into reverse. In Jesus' Name. Amen.

CHANGING PERSPECTIVE

For Reading and Meditation: Colossians 1:1–14

"...We are asking God that you may see things, as it were, from his point of view ..." (v. 9, J.B. Phillips)

We continue looking at some of our heavenly Father's ways – ways which, from a human perspective, seem strange and capricious, but when fully understood, are seen to contain the most profound purposes and the most astonishing wisdom.

THE ROAD TO TROUBLE

Another of our Father's ways is to take us by the hand and place us in situations where everything seems to go wrong. You would think that if God loved us as much as He says He does, He would lead us, not into troublesome situations but away from them. And as we know, difficulties have an uncanny way of coming together. For a while, everything goes pleasantly. Then suddenly, for no apparent reason, the skies are filled with thick and threatening clouds. A family member is struck down with sickness, business difficulties seem to shut one in on every side, and the whole world seems to tumble about one's ears.

At such times we cry out: why is God allowing this to happen to me? How can God say He loves me when He fails to answer my prayers and deliver me from such dark and difficult experiences? Ah, my friend, hold steady – there is a reason. It may appear on the surface of things that the Almighty has lost control – but nothing could be further from the truth. God never loses control of anything. If you could but penetrate the depths of the divine heart, you would see a purpose being worked out that would more than compensate for your feelings of uncertainty and doubt. You see things from your point of view – He sees things from His. Peace comes when you can change your perspectives to His.

God never loses control of anything.

Gracious Master, I would walk amid adversity with my head held high. But I cannot do this unless I bow my head at Your feet and learn Your ways. Help me see everything that happens to me from Your point of view. In Jesus' Name. Amen.

For Reading and Meditation: 2 Corinthians 9:6–15

*"And God is able to make all grace
abound to you ..." (v. 8)*

We continue considering the question: why does God sometimes lead us into situations where everything seems to go wrong? One answer to that question is this – it is God's way to focus more on development of our characters than on the development of our happiness. If you do not understand this – or are not willing to understand it – then you will find the hard and difficult situations in your life become even harder. Always remember this – the end of life is not happiness, but growth in character and spiritual achievement. And how can God develop our growth in character? There is only one way – He must put us in situations that are hard enough for us to sharpen our souls upon.

GROWTH STIMULATION

When I was an engineering student in my 'teens, I was taught that to get a sharp cutting edge on a machine tool, I needed to sharpen it against something that was much harder – an emery stone. Sometimes an emery stone would be faulty and too soft – hence ineffective. In pursuing the goal of growth in character, God is obliged to put us into situations which not only make growth possible, but stimulate it.

Here's something else we need to get hold of – whenever we find ourselves in a situation which looks as if it is too difficult to cope with, we can depend on it that all the resources we need to help us stand up to the pressure have already been provided through the foresight of a loving God. And where do we find these resources? In Jesus Christ. As one little boy put it: "Jesus is God's latchstring hung so low that anybody can reach it."

All the resources we need have already been provided.

O Father, what a thought to begin a day – You have provided everything for my growth in character. You don't just place me in difficult situations – You make available to me the grace I need to make them make me. I am so grateful. Amen.

UNIVERSITY TRAINING

For Reading and Meditation: James 1:1–12

"When all kinds of trials and temptations crowd into your lives ... don't resent them ... but welcome them as friends!" (v. 2, J.B. Phillips)

I f the chief goal which God has for us is not the development of our happiness but the development of our character, then it is obvious that He has to place us in situations where our characters can be perfected. And these situations must be sufficiently hard to sharpen our souls upon.

We live in a beautiful world, but a world that has been deeply damaged by sin. In some ways it is a hard world – one that is beset with earthquakes, tornadoes, volcanoes, disease-carrying germs, snakes, weeds and other things that have plagued mankind. Those who see only the problems say to themselves: God cannot be a loving and a perfect God, for if He were He would never have allowed His world to fall into such a state.

PROBLEMS OR OPPORTUNITIES

Others, however, take a different view. They see the hard side of the universe as an emery stone on which to sharpen their understanding. Instead of bemoaning the fact that disease-carrying germs exist, they set about the task of researching ways of combating them. When earthquakes come, they give themselves to finding ways of constructing buildings that can withstand them. Where they find weeds, they seek ways of getting rid of them. And what happens to such people? As they seek to improve the world around them, they succeed also in improving themselves.

It is the same in the Christian life. If we don't grow in character, it isn't because God has failed to set the stage for our growth; it is because we fail to sharpen our souls on the hard situation in which He places us. After all, the best university is the University of Adversity.

The best university is the University of Adversity.

O Father, help me to take any situation that is rasping and grating and use it to sharpen my soul. It is Your way to put character before happiness – help me to make it my way too. In Jesus' Name I ask it. Amen.

WHAT IF HE LEFT US ALONE?

For Reading and Meditation: Romans 8:26–39

"For from the very beginning God decided that those who came to him ... should become like his Son ..." (v. 29, TLB)

Suppose God left us alone and did not place us in situations which are perplexing and difficult – what would happen to us? Without something hard on which to sharpen our souls, we would be dull and lacking in initiative. We talked yesterday of those who respond to the challenge of a world in which there are earthquakes, tornadoes, disease-carrying germs and so on by seeking out ways to overcome the problems these things produce. But someone says: "This may be true, but dealing with a hard universe is one thing – dealing with hard people is another."

ENVIRONMENTAL DEVELOPMENT

Well, what about this environment of people? What do we do when God places us among difficult and irritating people? I am persuaded that this, too, is part of God's purpose to develop character within us. I know many who have grown to be better persons as a direct result of being surrounded by difficult and irritating people. If God has put you among people who try your patience, then decide that you will make this, not a groaning point, but a growing point.

I knew a woman in South Wales who married an extremely difficult man. He drank far too much, criticised her, shouted at her and did everything he could to make her life miserable. I asked her one day "How are you coping?" She replied, "My circumstances are helping me grow more like Jesus every day." I was staggered both by her words and by her radiant, integrated personality. Was this development of her character "in spite of" her environment and difficult situation? No, it was because of it. She made her environment make her.

More like Jesus every day.

My Father and my God, help me see that nothing can be greater than the development of character. And no character can be greater than the character of Jesus. Teach me how to make my circumstances make me more and more like Him. Amen.

For Reading and Meditation: I Peter 1:1–13

*"These have come so that your faith ...
may be proved genuine and may result in
praise, glory and honour ..." (v. 7)*

We are seeing that a hostile environment can be used by God to develop and deepen our characters. Just as an aircraft, when taking off, rises against the wind, so we can rise against the adverse winds of difficult situations to become more and more like Jesus Christ. This is God's way of building character in us, and if we fail to understand this principle, we will end up bitter rather than better.

THE EASY LIFE?

Can character be developed in serene and peaceful circumstances? Hardly. The story is told of a man who found himself in a position where every wish was immediately fulfilled and where every difficulty that confronted him was immediately resolved. He wanted a house – and there it was with servants at the door. He wanted a Rolls Royce and one appeared before him – complete with a uniformed chauffeur. He felt quite elated at the prospect of being able to have anything he wished for, but as time went on and more and more of his wishes were granted, the whole thing began to irritate him. He said to an attendant: "I want to get out of this situation as fast as I can. It is getting me down. I long to achieve something, to create something. I would rather be in hell than this." The attendant answered: "Where do you think you are?"

The planet on which we live contains such things as disease-carrying germs, snakes, earthquakes and so on, but awaiting our discovery are remedies for every one of these evils. In the midst of every difficulty and problem, there are always surprises in store for those who know where to look.

There are always surprises in store for those who know where to look.

O Father, when next I find myself in a situation where everything seems to be going wrong, I know exactly where I am going to look – I am going to look to YOU. Help me to turn everything to the deepening of my character. Amen.

GOD'S SOWING – OUR HARVEST

For Reading and Meditation: Job 23:1–12

"... When he has tested me,
I shall come forth as gold." (v. 10)

W e spend one more day meditating on the fact that one of God's ways is sometimes to lead us into situations where everything seems to go wrong.

A TALE OF TWO CHRISTIANS

I have often wondered why it is that two Christians in good health and with equal ability can go through the same set of difficult circumstances and yet react quite differently. One takes the difficult circumstances and sharpens his soul on them, thereby making himself more spiritually alert and responsive, while the other allows them to bring him down into defeat and discouragement.

The biggest single reason (in my opinion) is that one knows and understands the way God works, while the other does not. Knowing and understanding what God is about when we are placed in dark and difficult circumstances and when things are falling apart and nothing seems to be going right, enables us to look heavenward and say: "Lord, I know that You are working all things for my good, and through this situation You are going to make me more like Jesus Christ than I have ever been before. Therefore I will rise with You to see the whole thing from Your point of view."

God refines our natures, sensitises our souls and deepens our characters in this process. Troubles and trials stretch our hearts for new achievements, new usefulness and deeper character. Troubles plough the field for God's sowing, and our harvest – the harvest of character.

Troubles and trials stretch our hearts for new achievements.

O Father, I am so thankful that Your ways are not the ways of a despot who just likes to have his own way – they are the ways of a Deity who has our highest good at heart. I am so thankful. Amen.

"SLOW GROWTH"

For Reading and Meditation: Exodus 23:20–33

"Little by little I will drive them out before you,
until you have increased ..." (v. 30)

The thought I want to bring before you now can be best seen by comparing two different passages of Scripture. In our text for today, we read that God tells the children of Israel that when the time comes for them to enter the Promised Land, they will overcome their enemies – "little by little". In Deuteronomy 9:3, however, He says: "You will drive them out and annihilate them quickly". One passage says the enemies would be overcome slowly, the other says it would happen quickly – which is it to be? Is this a divine contradiction? No, for further investigation shows that some enemies would be overcome slowly, taking years, while others would fall quickly and be conquered in a day.

These texts reveal another aspect of God's ways – He purposes that we overcome some problems quickly, while others take a considerable length of time. Dr Lawrence Crabb, to whom I am indebted for this insight, calls it "the principle of slow growth".

INSTANT SOLUTIONS

I know that to some, this thought suggests spiritual defeatism. They will say: "God's power is great enough to enable us to overcome all our problems quickly. It is a denial of His might to suggest otherwise. When we are filled with the Spirit, all our problems can be dealt with quickly." I am afraid that one of the errors plaguing the Church at the moment is that of preaching a gospel of "instant solutions". I have heard it said: "Come to Christ and all your problems will be instantly resolved." It is not true. When we come to Christ, we have the potential for overcoming all our problems, but it is not true to say that they can all be instantly resolved. Some are resolved quickly, others slowly. Don't let anyone persuade you otherwise.

We have the potential for overcoming all our problems.

Gracious and loving heavenly Father, save me from the peril of expecting either too little or too much. Help me to gain a balanced and truly Biblical view of this issue. In Jesus' Name I pray. Amen.

GIANT-SIZED PROBLEMS

For Reading and Meditation: Joshua 11:1–20

"Joshua waged war against all these kings for a long time." (v. 18)

We continue meditating with the thought that some problems in our Christian lives are overcome quickly, while others take much longer to resolve. How can we differentiate between the two? Once again we compare two separate passages of Scripture – Joshua 11 and Joshua 15.

Joshua was given the task of leading the children of Israel into the Promised Land. In Joshua 11, verse 18 points out something very significant: "Joshua waged war against all these kings for a long time." Note the phrase – "a long time". Isn't this exactly what God had predicted? Had He not said that some enemies would take a long time to overcome and would be driven out "little by little"?

LITTLE AND LARGE

In Joshua 15:14, Caleb appears to have gained a quick victory over the three sons of Anak. You will remember that ten of the twelve spies who went into Canaan to evaluate the situation came back with a report that it contains "giants" (Num. 13:32 and 33) – among whom were the three sons of Anak. It was these giants who struck terror into the hearts of the ten spies and gave rise to their great unbelief. The problem which caused them to fear entering into the land yielded to a quick solution, while what they saw as a lesser problem took much longer to overcome.

One would think it ought to be the other way round.

Is there a principle here that we can bring over into everyday Christian living? I believe there is. As I look back, I can remember sometimes overcoming big problems with amazing ease, yet struggling for years with much less demanding or threatening problems. One would think it ought to be the other way round – smaller problems should be overcome quickly, while bigger ones take much longer. But for good reasons – it is not God's way.

O Father, what seems right to me may seem all wrong to You. If I am to succeed as a Christian, then I must look at things from Your viewpoint. Help me, Father. Amen.

GIANT-SIZED VICTORIES

For Reading and Meditation: I Samuel 17:32–51

"Your servant has killed both the lion and the bear; this uncircumcised Philistine will be like one of them ..." (v. 36)

Over the past few days our thoughts have focused around the fact that some problems we meet in the Christian life seem to be resolved quickly, while others take more time. We must now add one more thought: quick and sudden victories come only after we have wrestled for some time with smaller and lesser issues. We need to experience consistent victory in smaller issues before we can experience sudden victory in bigger issues.

HELPING THE DEPRESSED

I have often seen this principle at work in the lives of those who have been caught up in depression. What can we say to a Christian who is depressed? "In Jesus' name, claim the victory over your depression and command it to leave"? Or, "Put on a happy smile and go out to meet the world"? Such statements, generally speaking, are not helpful. Mostly they cause hurt and plunge the person deeper into depression. A better way is to encourage the depressed person to come to grips with the smaller issues of life and experience victory in them, before moving on to bigger and stronger challenges.

The approach I use is to say something like this: "Don't try to do too much too quickly. If you find it difficult to spend fifteen minutes praying or reading your Bible, then settle for just five minutes. If you don't feel like meeting or talking to many people in a day, then determine to talk to just one. If you don't feel like going for a long walk, then go only to the end of the street." By experiencing small victories in the day to day things, confidence is built up and people are then ready to face the bigger and greater challenges.

We need to experience consistent victory in smaller issues.

O Father, help me to come to grips with the smaller issues of my life, so that when I am confronted with the giant-sized problems, I will be prepared and ready. I ask this in Jesus' name. Amen.

WHY WE STRUGGLE

For Reading and Meditation: Proverbs 16:1–20

*"Pride goes before
destruction ..." (v. 18)*

We spend one more day meditating on the principle of "slow growth". We ask ourselves: what possible reason could God have had in planning for the Israelites to drive out some enemies slowly and other enemies quickly? The answer is found in a Scripture passage which we have already touched on – Exodus 23:29–30: "I will not drive them out from before you in one year, lest the land become desolate for lack of attention and the wild beasts multiply against you. Little by little I will drive them out ... until you have increased and are numerous enough to take possession of the land" (Amp. Bible).

DEPENDENT ON GOD

If God had cleared the Promised Land of all its occupants prior to Israel taking possession, the task of controlling it would have been too much for them. He therefore used the existing occupants to advance the purposes He had for His own people. Once we understand this principle – that God never acts arbitrarily but always purposefully – then we have the biggest single key to understanding His ways.

Had Israel taken possession of the land of Canaan without a struggle, they would have become proud, independent and self-reliant. God saw to it that they had enough resistance to keep them dependent upon Him. They advanced slowly, but in a way that worked out to their best advantage. Keep this in mind the next time you question why you still struggle with issues that you had hoped by now to have put behind you. God would rather have you panting than proud. While you struggle over the smaller issues now, our spiritual muscles are being built up, and though you do not know it, you are being prepared for the great victories that lie ahead.

God never acts arbitrarily, but always purposefully.

Father, I see that when I do not understand Your ways, I can so easily live against them – and get hurt. Once again I come to You with this simple but sincere prayer: Teach me Your ways, dear Lord. In Jesus' Name. Amen.

WHY? WHY? WHY?

For Reading and Meditation: Luke 11:1–13

"... how much more will your Father in heaven give the Holy Spirit to those who ask him!" (v. 13)

We move on to look at yet another of our heavenly Father's ways – one which, in my experience, has caused many of God's children a good deal of bewilderment and consternation. I refer to the habit that our heavenly Father has of appearing to withhold from us the very things He encourages us to pray for – things which we know for sure are within the scope and compass of His perfect will. Sometimes it looks as if, with one hand, God beckons us to ask Him for spiritual blessings, and with the other, He withholds them from us.

This characteristic of God used to puzzle me greatly when I first came into the Christian life. I used to ask myself: "Why is it that some Christians seem to get their prayers answered and others do not?" After thinking this through for a while, I came to the conclusion that perhaps it was because God had favourites, and that He liked some Christians better than others.

I held this erroneous belief for a long time until one day, the Lord opened up to me the passage that is before us today, and in it I discovered a principle which we shall look at in detail over the next few days.

WHAT GOD DELIGHTS TO DO

It is very important that we have a clear understanding of the magnanimity and large-heartedness that exists in God, for any doubt about this issue can sabotage our whole approach to prayer. If you are not absolutely sure that God is eager and willing to give, then you will not be able to approach Him with absolute confidence and this will affect your feelings about Him, your spiritual expectancy and your ability to receive.

God is always eager and willing to give.

O Father, help me at this point, for I see that if I take a wrong step here, I will take a wrong step everywhere. Burn deep into me the consciousness that You don't just give – You love to give. I am so thankful. Amen.

A FATHER – AND A FRIEND

For Reading and Meditation: Luke 12:22–34

"Do not fear, little flock, for it is your Father's good pleasure to give you the kingdom." (v. 32, NKJV)

We ended yesterday with the thought that any doubt we may have concerning God's desire to give will greatly affect our desire to ask – and in consequence, our readiness and willingness to receive. I believe myself that Jesus must have had this thought very much in mind when He told the story we looked at yesterday of the man who came at midnight to ask his friend for bread. Did you notice how Jesus preceded that story by giving His disciples a framework for prayer? We refer to it, of course, as "The Lord's Prayer", but notice how it begins: "Our Father in heaven ... Father! What a beautiful and exquisite word. It conjures up – or should conjure up – the thought of tender, loving care. You see, God is not just a Creator who creates something out of nothing: He is also a Father – with a father's love for His children.

ANOTHER PERSPECTIVE

Jesus knew, however, that for some the word "father" would have little meaning; they might not have had a loving father and thus there would be no loving content in the word. So He adds another perspective to the matter by talking about a man who came to his friend at midnight and asked for the loan of three loaves. See how Jesus, through carefully chosen words and phrases, builds up a picture of God – a God who is both a Father and a Friend. It is as if our Lord is saying: "If you have any problems about not receiving the things that you feel you ought to be receiving, then understand that the difficulties are not on God's side: He is a loving Father and a concerned Friend." If we don't get this right, then we won't get anything right. Prayer that doesn't begin here doesn't begin.

Prayer that doesn't begin here doesn't begin.

My Father and my God, I see that unless I begin right, I cannot expect to finish right. Once again, I ask You to give me an even clearer and sharper vision of Your willingness and eagerness to give. In Jesus' Name. Amen.

"HOW MUCH MORE ..."

For Reading and Meditation: Romans 8:28–39

"He who did not spare his own Son ...
how will he not also, along with him, graciously
give us all things?" (v. 32)

Our search continues for answers to the problem of why God sometimes withholds from us the very things He encourages us to pray for – things which we know for sure are in line with His will. We have seen that the reason is not because God is mean, niggardly or tight-fisted. Jesus told us that God is both a loving Father and a concerned Friend. So let there be no doubt about it – the Almighty loves nothing better than to give good gifts to His children.

BOUNDLESS GENEROSITY

Listen once again to the way Jesus puts it: "How much more will your heavenly Father give the Holy Spirit to those who ask him!" (Luke 11:13, NKJV). Note the words – "how much more". What gives an earthly father more delight than to be able to give to his child something he knows will be good for it and bring it endless joy? It is the same with our heavenly Father – only a million times more.

An old lady in a church I once had the care of approached me and asked me for my help in straightening out her prayer life. She told me that she never got any answers to her prayers, and when I asked her to tell me how she saw prayer and what sort of picture she had of the God to whom she was praying, she said: "I picture God standing in the midst of heaven with His hands behind His back, and it is my job, through prayer, to try to get behind Him, prise open His hands and wrest from Him the things I need." Can you see how difficult it would be for a person like this, with such a faulty concept of God, to approach Him with confidence and trust? She wasn't praying to God – she was praying to a caricature.

> *The Almighty loves nothing better than to give.*

Father, it is clear that the way I see You will determine the way I approach You. Cleanse my mind and my heart of any misconceptions and misunderstandings that may be within me. Help me to see, Lord – really see. In Jesus' Name. Amen.

NOT THE WORDS OF OUR LIPS

For Reading and Meditation: Matthew 7:1–12

"Ask and it will be given to you; seek and you will find; knock and the door will be opened to you." (v. 7)

Now that we have cleared away any doubts about God's willingness and eagerness to give, we must go on to ask another important question: if God is such a joyous giver, why is it that so often we ask but do not receive? Isn't it true that sometimes we pray for things that are valid and legitimate – like a deeper encounter with the Holy Spirit – and life stays pretty much the way it is. We ask for more power, but no answer is given. Why? I believe the answer lies in these words of Jesus: "I say to you, ask, and it will be given to you; seek, and you will find; knock, and it will be opened to you" (Luke 11:9, NKJV).

A DEEPENING DESIRE

It is quite clear from what our Lord is saying here that there are three levels of spiritual longing and desire – asking, seeking and knocking. The usual interpretation of this text is that if, after we have asked, we do not receive, then we must become more intensive and determined in our praying – and seek. Then, if after having intensified our praying, we still have not received, we must become still more intense and determined – and knock.

I wonder, however, whether our Lord was thinking here, not so much of intensity of action as intensity of desire. You see, prayer depends not so much on the words that cross our lips as on the desire that is in our hearts. Some have such deep spiritual desire within them that all they need to do is ask – and they receive. Others use all the right words and phrases, but their desire does not match their words. Thus they have to go down to deeper levels of searching until they find the place where the desire of their hearts matches the prayer of their lips.

Prayer depends on the desire that is in our hearts.

Gracious and loving Father, bring me to the place where my desire to receive is as strong in quality, if not in quantity, as Your desire to give. Then I know that "all things are possible". In Jesus' Name I pray. Amen.

INNER – NOT OUTER

For Reading and Meditation: Matthew 5:1–16

"Blessed are those who hunger and thirst for righteousness, for they will be filled." (v. 6)

We spend one last meditating on the thought that our ability to receive from God is not determined by the prayers of our lips alone, but by the depth and degree of spiritual desire that resides in our heart.

REACHING FOR THE SKY

I sometimes think that the Church has missed its way in relation to its understanding of spiritual desire. We mistake desire for demand, and this is why we tend to see prayer as making demands upon God rather than laying hold on what He delights to give by way of spiritual desire. There is a place for making demands in prayer, of course, as the great prayers of the Old Testament show, but prayer is more than a demand – it is also a desire. And when our desire to receive matches, even only feebly, God's desire to give – then the sky's the limit.

Some Christians see in the words "ask", "seek" and "knock" the thought that we must bombard the gates of heaven with our petitions in order to overcome God's reluctance. Others, however – and I hope you are one – see prayer, not as overcoming God's reluctance, but laying hold on His highest willingness. But remember – the intensity He is looking for is not intensity of action, but of desire – not outer action but inner action.

When we ask and do not receive, we should examine ourselves on that level to see whether the desire of our hearts matches the desire of our lips. If it doesn't, then we must assume that we need to examine and intensify our spiritual desires at a deeper level of seeking. And if nothing happens at that level, then we go deeper still – and knock. This process is our heavenly Father's way of making sure that we learn not to take things for granted.

We mistake desire for demand.

O Father, I see that behind all Your withholdings is a desire for my spiritual maturity – so that my longing to receive matches Your longing to give. And help me learn never to take things for granted – but with gratitude. In Jesus' Name. Amen.

UNEXPECTED PLACES

For Reading and Meditation: Genesis 28:1–22

"... 'How awesome is this place! This is none other than the house of God; this is the gate of heaven!' " (v. 17)

Another intriguing characteristic of our heavenly Father is the way He has of revealing Himself through the most ordinary means and in the most unexpected places.

HEAVEN ON EARTH

God met Jacob on the bare and barren hillside and under the stars. Who would ever expect to meet God in a desolate and unfrequented wilderness, unknown to worship and unhallowed by praise? Yet it was there that God held tryst with Jacob. I am convinced myself that although God's prime way of meeting us is in and through the Scriptures, He is also constantly seeking to meet us in the common and unexpected places of life – through ordinary things and ordinary moments. He does not wait for what we call the "grander moments", but makes the ordinary and the commonplace into the grand. And if we are not prepared for this, we can miss many a moment of spiritual exhilaration and discovery.

I remember on one occasion standing in Trafalgar Square, London, at a time when it was crowded with holidaymakers and visitors. I certainly never expected to hear God speak to me there – yet He did. That day the well-known fountains that are in the Square were dry due to a failure of the pumps, and as I looked upon the scene God said to me: "This is how your life will become unless you maintain constant contact with Me." From that day to this, I have tried to keep my heart open to everything that is around me – and my life has been all the richer for it.

He makes the ordinary and the common-place into the grand.

O Father, while not ceasing to look for You in Your Word, the Bible, help me to discover You also in the ordinary and the unexpected moments of life. Make the commonplace glorious for me today. In Jesus' Name I pray. Amen.

MINGLING WITH EARTHLY CLAY

For Reading and Meditation: Matthew 13:44–58

" 'Isn't this the carpenter's son? ...' " (v. 55)

The thought we are pursuing at the moment – that God is constantly seeking to meet us in the common and unexpected places of life – will, I know, present a problem to many. Some will say that the only place we find God is in Scripture, and outside of that one and only infallible source, any revelation of God must be treated with suspicion and distrust. I have much sympathy with that line of thinking, for I know many who, having no confidence in Scripture, have sought to find God in the ordinary and the commonplace, only to come out with some of the strangest and weirdest interpretations of God and His ways I have ever heard. We must watch that we do not interpret Scripture by life's circumstances, but we must interpret life's circumstances by Scripture.

GOD SHARED OUR LIFE

Having made that point clear, let me go on now to say once again that it is in our spiritual interests to develop an awareness of God in the ordinary and the commonplace. George MacDonald said: "It is so easy to deny the nobility of something just because it mingles with our earthly clay." How true – and to do that is to miss part of the meaning of the Incarnation.

Listen to the way one preacher makes this same point: "When God came to earth in the person of His Son, He came as no hermit dwelling in a solitary place and giving Himself at rare intervals only to the few; He was born into the intimate home life of an ordinary family in Nazareth. When His ministry began, He kept Himself for the most part in the crowded ways of men; He dressed as they dressed, spoke with a Galilean accent, knew hunger and heartache and weariness and shared their life in everything but sin."

Develop an awareness of God in the ordinary.

Lord Jesus, I am so grateful that while never ceasing to be what You had always been – true God – You became what You had never been before – true Man. You are as wonderful in Your humiliation on You are in Your exaltation. Amen.

THE ORDINARINESS OF JESUS

For Reading and Meditation: John 14:1–14

"... 'Have I been with you so long, and yet you have not known me ... He who has seen me has seen the Father ...'" (v. 9, NKJV)

In the passage before us today, Philip seemed completely to miss the fact that the One with whom he had rubbed shoulders for so long was, in fact, God of very God. We tend to come down hard on Philip for his failure to recognise Jesus aright. When he made his request, "Show us the Father, and it is sufficient for us", he probably had in mind the experience of Moses and believed that God could be seen only in some dazzling vision. Perhaps he hoped that Jesus would reward them with a similar experience and that their doubts would be shrivelled up in a dramatic and glorious encounter with the living God.

It does not surprise me that Philip failed to recognise Jesus as God, for human nature is always more attracted to the spectacular than the truly great. This error is not peculiar to Philip and the disciples; many make the same mistake today. They seek at a distance the God who stands before them at the door of their heart. They wonder how to ascend the ladder that reaches from earth to heaven and wait for it to be thrown down to them while, in fact, the foot of that ladder is right beside them.

A DAY OF DECISION

God stands at the door of your heart.

Those of you who are Christians will bear with me, I know, if I pause to ask those reading these lines and who have never committed their lives to Christ to reach out to God. The ladder is at your side. Ask God to come into your life, to forgive your sin and make you His child. Take my word for it – all you need do is reach out to Him. He will do the rest. Do it today. No – do it now. I urge you: receive Him now – today.

O God, I have looked for the ladder of salvation to drip out of the skies, yet now I see it as at my side. I have looked for You afar off – yet You have been so near. I reach out now – with all my heart. Save me. In Jesus' Name I ask it. Amen.

ORDINARY WORDS

For Reading and Meditation: Acts 10:1–23

"… the Holy Spirit said to him,
'Three men have come to see you. Go down and
meet them …'" (vv. 19–20, TLB)

Not only does God involve Himself in the ordinary moments and the ordinary circumstances of life, but there are times when the words He speaks to us seen ordinary too. I was brought up to believe that if ever God spoke to me, He would do so in the language of the King James version. That is why the first words I ever heard Him say to me came as a complete and utter shock. I was staggered by their ordinariness.

NEARER THAN WE THINK

Permit me to tell you about it. I had only been a Christian a few months, and one day, while kneeling in prayer at a Holy Communion service, I was pondering on how much Christ meant to me. As I waited, I heard God's voice ring out inside my soul – "And you, my dear Selwyn, mean much more to Me." The words were very ordinary – no "thee's" or "thou's" – but I have no language to describe the effect they had upon me. The fact that God had spoken to me in ordinary words reached deep into my heart and mind. I confess that the very memory of that event is causing a tear to trickle down my face as I write.

The great Baptist preacher C.H. Spurgeon was fond of quoting the story of his housemaid, who told him that on the first day she began to work for him, she knelt by her bedside and dedicated her household duties to God. When she had finished her prayer, God spoke to her and said: "Remember to sweep under the mats." Oh, yes, it is ordinary – absurdly so. But then God is concerned with ordinary things. Duties matter to Him. In the common moments of the day, God is there. Don't search afar; don't wait for some blinding vision. Look for Him in the ordinary ways of life. He is nearer to you than you think.

In the common moments of the day, God is there.

O Father, help me to make the most of every moment by seeing and sensing that You are in every moment. Show me how to walk down familiar pathways and see unfamiliar things; to discover You in the ordinary and the mundane. Amen.

SHAVINGS OF SOLID GOLD

For Reading and Meditation: Ecclesiastes 9:1–19

*"Whatever your hand finds to do, do it
with your might ..." (v. 10, NKJV)*

God reveals Himself, not only in the sublime but also in
the simple; not just in the "grand moments" of life but
in the ordinary moments too. It's the way our heavenly
Father likes to do things, and if we fail to comprehend His
style, we will deprive ourselves of many spiritual discoveries.
So let me urge you, as I urge myself, to cultivate the eye that
finds God in ordinary things. Some of you are expecting a
blinding revelation of God to come to you in the future –
and it may well happen – but don't focus so much on what
may lie ahead that you miss what God is doing in your
ordinary moments.

I read somewhere an old legend of an angel who came
one evening to the brink of a river and asked the boatman
to ferry him across. When they reached the farther shore, the
angel rewarded the boatman with what appeared to be a
handful of wooden shavings and in disgust, the boatman
threw them into the river. The next morning he found one
of those shavings left in the bottom of his boat and on
examining it closely, found it was not a shaving of wood but
a shaving of gold. My friend, the ordinary moments of
life pass quickly – don't see them as worthless shavings to be
thrown away in pique at receiving nothing better. Look at
them more closely, and you will see that they are solid gold.
As Keble puts it:

*If on our daily course our mind
Be set to hallow all we find
New treasure still of countless price
God will provide for sacrifice.*

*Cultivate
the eye that
finds God
in ordinary
things.*

O God my Father, now that I have caught something of the way
in which You delight to invade the ordinary, help me to look
more closely at my ordinary moments. For only then will I see
that they are made, not of wood, but of gold. Amen.

"IN HIS TIME"

For Reading and Meditation: Ecclesiastes 3:1–15

"He has made everything beautiful in its time ..." (v. 11)

What more can we learn about our heavenly Father's strange but wondrous ways? This – it is His way to finish and perfect everything He begins. Our text for today sums up that truth most beautifully when it says that He makes everything beautiful in its time. Notice the last three words – "in its time". Some things on which God is working may not look very beautiful at the moment, but they will – in time. A chorus Christians love to sing, born out of the verse that is before us today, says:

> *In His time, in His time,*
> *He makes all things beautiful*
> *In His time.*
> *Lord, please show me every day*
> *As You're teaching me Your way*
> *That You'll do just what You say*
> *In Your time.*

WITH UTMOST PATIENCE

What needless suffering and anxiety we carry within us because we fail to understand that although God dwells in eternity, He is working out His purposes here on earth in accordance with time. He could bring about major changes in our lives in a single moment – and of course He often does – but usually His way is to work painstakingly through dark and difficult situations – taking His time. A wise man once said: "The greatest lesson we can learn from life is that God is never in a hurry." I agree. He is the most patient Being in the universe. Believe me, we will save ourselves a good deal of personal pain and irritation when we learn to have patience with the patience of God.

"God is never in a hurry."

My Father and my God, You are so poised, so persistent, so patient. It is Your way. I see that Your long-range purposes take time. Help me to be as patient as You are in waiting for them to come to pass. In Jesus' Name. Amen.

RIGHT ON TIME

For Reading and Meditation: Psalm 31:1–24

"My times are in your hand …" (v. 15)

We quoted yesterday the words of a wise man who said: "The greatest lesson we can learn from life is that God is never in a hurry." And if we don't learn that lesson, we leave ourselves open to a good deal of irritation and frustration.

THE GREATEST MYSTERY

An example of how slow and unhurried God is in working out His purposes can be seen in Christ's first advent. The promise that one day God would send someone to overturn the effects of the Fall was, as you know, given to Adam and Eve in the Garden of Eden. Later it was reiterated in many different ways – through the prophets, through the patriarchs, through the Tabernacle and Temple sacrifices and so on. Century after century rolled by – and still no Christ. "Give us a Christ", cried out the masses of humanity as they sensed their need of someone to right the world's wrongs. But the heavens remained mute and silent. "Give us a Christ", cried the nation of Israel as they saw the stones of their beloved Jerusalem overturned. But century after century came and went – and still no Christ.

Then, when it looked as if God had forgotten His promise and no prophet had spoken in Israel for 400 years, the heavens responded and a Word was spoken – Jesus. A little bundle of life moved in a crib in Bethlehem and the greatest mystery of the ages took shape – "the Word became flesh and dwelt among us". Did Jesus arrive too late? Some might think so. But what does the Bible say? "When the fullness of the time had come, God sent forth His Son" (Gal. 4:4, NKJV). He came not too early, not too late – but right on time.

A Word was spoken – Jesus.

Gracious and loving heavenly Father, You have made me in such a way that I can only give myself wholly to someone I trust. And if I cannot trust You – then who can I trust? You have my life – help me to trust You more. Amen.

GOD IS IN CHARGE

For Reading and Meditation: Job 28:12–28

"God understands its way,
And he knows its place." (v. 23, NKJV)

Here ow much we miss when we fail to see and sense God's timing in our earthly affairs. If we look at our lives strictly as they are laid out before us and lose sight of the fact that God is at work, we can fall prey to doubt and disillusionment. How often have we heard people say, when things just don't seem to be working out for them: "I find it difficult to believe there is a loving purpose at work in my life. If there is, then why do things take so long to come together?"

SEEN THROUGH GOD'S EYES

H.G. Wells once declared, in a wild and bitter mood, that if there was a personal God behind this shambles of a universe, he would spit in his face! It is easy to toss that statement aside and regard it as blasphemous, but I have sat with many committed Christians who have gone through one tragedy after another, and though they would not have used the words of H.G. Wells, they certainly share his sentiment. A man I once knew very well and whom I regarded as a fine Christian stood up in my presence and shook his fist at God, saying: "God, You don't know what You are doing."

What can save us from falling into such a mood and using wild, frenzied words of defiance and doubt? I know of nothing more effective than the conviction that He makes everything beautiful in its time. The picture that you see now as you look at your life may not be very beautiful, but when you see it through His eyes, in His time, the picture takes on a perspective that is just out of this world. You will see purpose in tragedy, reason in calamity and meaning in everything. No matter what your circumstances are like at the moment, never, never lose hope. God is still in charge.

You will see meaning in everything.

O Father, You know how easy this is to say, but how hard to hold on to when I am hurting. Yet I know it to be true. I acknowledge my need for greater dependency upon You. Help me, dear Lord. In Jesus' Name. Amen.

MAKING ALL THINGS WORK

For Reading and Meditation: Romans 8:28

"And we know that all things work together for good to those who love God, to those who are the called according to his purpose." (NKJV)

The verse that is before us today is, as long-time readers of *Every Day with Jesus* know, a favourite of mine and they expect me to comment on it from time to time. If I was asked to give the two texts of Scripture that God has used most in my life, this would be one – the other being John 3:16. The key phrase in this verse is "work together". The verse is careful not to say that all things are good, for quite clearly, all things are not good. Sin is not good. Death and bereavement are not good. An earthquake or a flood is not good. All things are good only as they work together for God's purpose.

IT'S STILL TRUE!

Some time ago, while in the United States, I drove past a college in Richmond, Virginia, and I remembered reading the story of a professor there who was asked by his students after he had addressed the morning assembly on the theme of Romans 8:28: "But, Professor, you don't really believe that all things work together for good – all the pain and misery – do you?" The professor replied: "The things in themselves may not be good, but God can make them work together for good."

That afternoon, he and his wife were out driving when they collided with another care. His wife was killed instantly and he himself was left a cripple. One day, several weeks later, he sent for the president of the college and said: "Tell my students that Romans 8:28 still holds good." When, just one year later the professor died, his students had this verse from Romans inscribed on his tombstone. At the ceremony, a local newspaper reporter asked them why they had done this. They replied: "It was inscribed in his convictions: why not on his gravestone?"

All things are good only as they work together for God's purpose.

O Father, I see that if I can have this truth inscribed in my convictions, then I will be able to face everything that comes with fortitude and faith. So day by day, burn these words more deeply into my spirit. In Jesus' Name I pray. Amen.

YES – EVERYTHING

For Reading and Meditation: I Corinthians 2:6–16

"… 'Eye has not seen, nor ear heard, nor have entered into the heart of man the things which God has prepared for those who love him.' " (v. 9, NKJV)

We continue meditating on the fact that it is our Father's way to finish and perfect everything He begins. But He does this over a period of time. Ah – there's the rub. Some of us wish God would hurry up with His plans and not take so long to get them accomplished – especially when those plans cross and conflict with our personal aims and desires.

THE FINISHED PRODUCT

If you struggle with the truth of God's timing, then here's something you have got to get hold of – you may not live to see God's time completely fulfilled. You may live beyond the allotted three score years and ten, attain many of your personal goals and ambitions and yet die before the full programme of God has reached its ultimate and completed purpose. But His promise stands – He will make everything beautiful in its time. You see, our problem is that we get our attention focused on the wrong things. We see the strange-looking cocoon; God sees the finished butterfly. We see the ugly strands; He sees the finished design. We see today – He sees tomorrow.

Let the text that I have given you over these past few days – "He makes everything beautiful in its time" – sink deeply into your spirit. In my Bible, I have underlined the word "everything". I believe God would not have said "every-thing" unless He meant everything. This means that all your losses, failures, brokenness, heartaches, fears, childhood hurts, fragmented dreams, lost loves, financial reverses, sickness and illnesses will be made beautiful in time. Without God, life is pointless and purposeless; with Him, it will ultimately make sense.

His promise still stands.

Dear, loving heavenly Father, I am thrilled beyond words to realise I am caught up in something that has a cosmic guarantee. Everything that has happened to me will be made beautiful in its time. Hallelujah!

INFLUENCES LIVE ON

For Reading and Meditation: Hebrews 11:1–16

"… through faith, though he is dead, he still speaks." (v. 4, NASB)

We stay with this thought that we may not live to see God's time completely fulfilled. During the eighteen years I spent as a pastor, I had occasion to witness the death of many Christians. Sometimes I would be called out in the middle of the night just to hold their hand and read to them from the Word of God as they passed into the presence of the Lord.

A GLORIOUS PATTERN

Oftentimes they would say to me: "But there are so many things I have left undone. I wish God would give me a few more years to complete some of the things I want to do for Him." Then I would read to them the text I have been bringing before you during the last few days: "He makes everything beautiful in its time." I would say something like this: "The work you have started will not end when you die. It will still go on and God will see that it will be not limited by your crossing over into His presence. The things that have happened to you will be taken by Him and woven into a glorious pattern so that when you see it in eternity, you will realise that it is our Father's way to finish and perfect everything He has begun."

I hope the words that brought comfort to them will bring comfort to you know – especially those of you who feel that your life's work is coming to an end. Has life sped by so quickly that you feel there are many things left undone? Are you somewhat saddened when you think that the sand in the hourglass is running out? Then take heart – God will finish and perfect everything He has started in your life, even if He has to extend the influences of it into the next generation.

> *The work you have started will not end when you die.*

O Father, what delight and comfort it brings me to know that when my life here on earth ends, You will go on working on what I started and will not stop until You bring it to perfection. I am so grateful. Amen.

DEATH CANNOT CHEAT HIM

For Reading and Meditation: Philippians 1:1–11

"… he who has begun a good work in you will complete it until the day of Jesus Christ." (v. 6, NKJV)

I t is our Father's way to finish and perfect everything He begins. Everything God does is painstaking and thorough. He does nothing with shallowness or superficiality. The Almighty is not interested in glueing on to our lives the thin veneers that are so typical of much modern furniture. He carves things that are solid and permanent – things that will outlast time and live on through eternity.

COMPLETE AND PERFECT

Charles Swindoll puts it like this: "Everything God does is thorough. It's never too little, never too late … it's never too much, never too early and there's never anything missing." So drop your anchor down deep into the thoroughness of God. The Almighty is going to do a complete and perfect job on your life and He will not allow anything, not even your death, to cheat Him. I have known many people, and I am sure you do too, whose lives still go on speaking and working for God long after they have passed on. It is as if God says: "I am not able to perfect My purposes in this life over the period of one generation, so I need to extend them into another."

I am thinking as I write of a friend of mine, now with the Lord, whose life seemed to consist of one failure after another. Yet amazingly, those failures drew his family to-gether in such a way that out of them came a dedication and commitment to Christ that brought two sons into the Christian ministry and put a daughter on the mission field. I dare to believe that in eternity, the picture my friend will see is not one of failure but success, for He makes everything beautiful in its time.

Drop your anchor down deep into the thorough-ness of God.

My Father and my God, I bow in adoration before the wonder of the fact that what You start, You finish – even if You have to go on working beyond death to complete it. Accept my deepest gratitude, dear Father – from the bottom of my heart. Amen.

GOD INSISTS ON IT

For Reading and Meditation: Isaiah 42:1–16

*"... I will not give my glory
to another ..." (v. 8)*

We come now to the final stage of our meditations. The last "way" of God we examine comes out of our text for today; it is the way God has of insisting that all the glory must be given to Himself. I must confess that at one time, this particular aspect of God used to trouble me greatly. We all tend to despise those people who, having been involved in some achievement, want to hog the limelight and are unwilling to share the credit with others who have also had some part to play in it – even though a small one.

TO GOD BE THE GLORY

Many Christians have stumbled over this aspect of God wanting to have all the glory and honour for Himself – the great writer C. S. Lewis among them. He says in one of his books that when he first began to draw near to belief in God, he found it difficult to understand why He insisted on being continually honoured and praised. He wrote: "It was hideously like saying: 'What I most want is to be told that I am good and great.'"

He went on to say also that there were certain texts in Scripture, particularly in the Psalms, which seemed to suggest that those petitioning God were caught up in a kind of bargaining relationship with Him which proceeded along these lines: "Lord, You do this for me, and I will give You the glory that You seem to find such delight in receiving." Here's one such text, for example: "Help us ... For the glory of your name" (Psa. 79:9, NKJV).

Of course, C. S. Lewis came to see that this was not the case, but it goes to show how easy it is to misunderstand and misinterpret Scripture when we fail to see the reasons that lie behind God's ways.

*How easy
it is to mis-
understand
and mis-
interpret
Scripture.*

Gracious Lord and Master, You have made me in Your image, but so often I try to make You in my image. Help me once and for all to stop looking at Your ways in the light of my ways, but to look at my ways in the light of Yours. Amen.

WORTHY OF ALL HONOUR

For Reading and Meditation: Hebrews 1:1–14

Wcome now to face the question: why does God insist on taking all the honour and glory to Himself? Firstly – because He has a right to it. Can anyone deny Him that? God is not just the originator of our universe, but, as our text for today shows, He is constantly at work supporting and upholding it. And what a universe it is! Our scientists tell us that in relation to the myriads of other orbs that are in space, the earth on which we live is like a single grain of sand among all the other grains of sand on all the sea-shores of the world. They further tell us that if our earth were to fall out of its orbit and spin away into space, it would make no more impact than the dropping of a pea into the Pacific Ocean.

ALMIGHTY AND ALL-SUFFICIENT

Why am I using these word pictures? To show you that the God who created all this is a great and mighty Creator. Conceivably the world might have been constructed on a lesser scale. God could have designed just one solar system – and the universe would still be immense and amazing. The fact that He made it as large as it is points to the greatness of His mind and the greatness of His power in bringing it into being.

What is it all for? What purpose does it serve? To what does it point? It points to the fact that God is almighty and all-sufficient. This one fact alone ought to be enough to convince us that He has earned the right to unceasing honour and eternal praise. Everything we have – breath, life, reason and so on – we have received from Him. Dare we take any of the credit for the creation? Or give the glory to another but our great and glorious God?

Everything we have we have from him.

My Father and my God, You will have no argument from me. Help me at this very moment to focus all the appreciation that resides within my heart and direct it toward You. I honour and revere You, dear Father – more than words can convey. Amen.

"NOT FULLY AWAKE"

For Reading and Meditation: Revelation 4:1–11

"... Day and night they never stop saying:
'Holy, holy, holy is the Lord God Almighty ...'" (v. 8)

Another reason why God insists on us bringing to Him all the honour and the glory is this – the more we do this, the more we complete ourselves. Forgive me for taking you through what might be for some a complex train of reasoning, but I promise you, the effort you put forth to grasp the point I am making will bring its own spiritual reward.

A DOUBLE DEPRIVATION

Imagine a person standing in front of a beautiful painting or an exquisite piece of art and saying to themselves: "My, this is an admirable piece of work" – what do they mean? They mean it deserves admiration, and that admiration is the only correct, adequate and appropriate response to it. But then someone like myself comes along, who has little experience or interest in pieces of art, and I simply glance at it, yawn and pass on.

The person who is riveted to the spot by the beauty of the piece of art looks at me in amazement and says: "Don't you appreciate what is before you?" I say, "I'm afraid I don't really see much in it." The person then replies: "If you cannot see the genius in this, then there is a world you know nothing about – you are not fully awake. And with all your experience of people and of writing, there is a part of you that is incomplete. Not to appreciate what ought to be appreciated will leave you inwardly deprived."

I would have no difficulty in accepting that argument, for although I have little personal interest in objects of art, I know intellectually that not to appreciate something that deserves to be appreciated results in some loss to me. In failing to honour God as God, I do not just deprive Him, I also deprive myself.

The more we do this, the more we complete ourselves.

O Father, thank You for showing me that it is only when I focus on celebrating Your worth that I come awake. Help me always to be ready to ascribe to You all honour and glory, for I see that the more I do that, the more awake I shall be. Amen.

IT IS SO RIGHT

For Reading and Meditation: Psalm 92:1–15

"It is good to give thanks to the Lord,
And to sing praises to your name, O Most High." (v. 1, NKJV)

We must dwell a little longer on the thought that one of the reasons why God insists on us giving Him honour and glory is because He knows that by so doing, we complete ourselves. C.S. Lewis articulates this thought far more effectively than I ever could when he says: "He [God] is that Object to admire which is simply to be awake, to have entered the real world; not to appreciate which is to have lost the greatest experience and, in the end, to have lost all." A closely reasoned and complex statement but one well worth rolling around in your mind through the spare moments of this day.

A FAINT REFLECTION

He goes on to say that the lives of those who are tone-deaf, have never been in love, never known true friendship, never cared for good books, never enjoyed the feel of the morning air, are somewhat incomplete, and these deficiencies are a faint reflection of a life in which there is no attempt to live for the glory of God. I urge you to latch on to this thought, for once you see that the reason why God insists on your giving Him all the honour and glory is not that you might gratify some appetite in Him, but rather that you might become more whole and complete, then never again will you want to draw back from giving Him what He asks.

Never draw back from giving Him what He asks.

I have met many Christians who secretly thought that the text: "My glory I will not give to another" implied that God is a Being who craves for glory in the same way that a vain woman searches for compliments or a new author sends his books to people who have never heard of him. But that, as you know now, is not His reason – He desires it, not just because it is right for Him, but also because it is right for us.

O Father, not only is it good to give You honour and praise – but it feels so right. Somehow everything within me is drawn toward health as I focus on giving You the glory You deserve. I am so thankful. Amen.

For Reading and Meditation: Isaiah 43:1–7

*"Everyone who is called by my name,
whom I created for my glory ..." (v. 7)*

We look at yet another reason why God insists on us giving Him the glory – because in commanding us to glorify Him, God is inviting us to enjoy Him. The Westminster Catechism says that man's chief end is "to glorify God and enjoy Him forever". Fully to glorify God is fully to enjoy Him and fully to enjoy Him is fully to glorify Him.

PERFECT BLISS

Follow me carefully at this point: if we could perfectly ascribe glory to someone or something, that is, utterly express or get out the upsurge of appreciation that rises within us, then indeed the object would be fully appreciated and honoured and in the giving of that honour, our own delight would attain perfect development. And the worthier the object, the more intense this delight would be. If it were possible for us in this present state perfectly to focus on and perfectly delight in giving God the honour and glory which He deserves, and to keep this up moment by moment, then we would experience a bliss that could not be described in words.

This is perhaps the nearest idea we will ever get as to what heaven is like – a state and a place in which redeemed sinners focus on bringing glory to the everlasting Creator and in the glorifying of whom they experience in themselves perfect blessedness and bliss. Meanwhile, here on earth "we are tuning our instruments in anticipation of the perfect symphony". The tuning up of the orchestra can itself be a delight, but only to those who can in some measure anticipate what is to follow. Believe me, our glorifying of the Lord here on earth is but a trickle compare to the full flood that will flow out of us when we see Him face to face.

God is inviting us to enjoy Him.

O Father, my heart longs for the day when I can give You perfect honour and praise. Meanwhile, help me to tune up my spirit, my instrument of worship, so that I shall be ready for the heavenly symphony. Amen.

"THE FAMILY STYLE"

For Reading and Meditation: Psalm 18:20–32

"As for God, his way is perfect …" (v. 30)

We end our meditations where we began by affirming that without a knowledge of our Father's ways, we can soon find ourselves beset by worry, frustration and fear. The eight ways of God around which this study has been built are, however, only some of our Father's special characteristics. He has many others.

THE FATHER'S WAY

Let me bring the ones that have occupied our attention in these meditations before you once again in the form of a final review. It is God's way (1) to test before He entrusts; (2) to reveal, reverse and then restore; (3) to place us in situations where everything seems to go wrong; (4) to arrange for some problems to be overcome quickly, but others to be overcome slowly; (5) to withhold from us the very things He encourages us to pray for; (6) to reveal Himself in the most ordinary of ways and in the most unexpected places; (7) to finish and perfect everything He begins; and (8) to insist on having all the glory for Himself.

Knowing and understanding these eight ways of God will acquaint you with the "family style" – our heavenly Father's way of doing things. Then, at some time in the future, when you come up against a "way" of God than seems strange and mysterious, you will be able to relax and say to yourself: "I know enough about my Father to realise that when I cannot see or understand the reason for His actions, He is pursuing a way that makes perfect sense." You will find, as I have found, that it is not easy to lose in the dark the principles you have discovered in the light.

He is pursuing a way that makes perfect sense.

My Father, I am grateful for all I have learned about You and Your ways during these past days and weeks. Help me to carry these thoughts with me into the future so that never again will I be at the mercy of circumstances. In Jesus' Name I ask it. Amen.